Pretend
the World

Books by Kathryn Kysar

Poetry

Dark Lake (Loonfeather Press, 2002)
Pretend the World (Holy Cow! Press, 2011)

Essays

Editor, *Riding Shotgun: Women Write About Their Mothers*
(Minnesota Historical Society Press, Borealis Books, 2008)

Pretend
the World

Poems by

Kathryn Kysar

Holy Cow! Press :: Duluth, Minnesota :: 2011

Author photograph by Joe Szurszewski.

Cover painting by Julie Buffalohead. "My Little Friends" (2008), 19.75 x 25.5 inches, mixed media on paper. Copyright © artist and Bockley Gallery, and used by permission.

Library of Congress Cataloging-in-Publication Data

Kysar, Kathryn, 1960-
Pretend the world : poems / by Kathryn Kysar.—1st ed.
    p. cm.
ISBN 978-0-9823545-4-4 (alk. paper)
I. Women—Poetry. I. Title.
PS3611.Y73P74 2011
811'.6—dc22   2011000912

Holy Cow! Press books are distributed to the trade by Consortium Book Sales & Distribution, c/o Perseus Distribution, 1094 Flex Drive, Jackson, Tennessee 38301.

For personal inquiries, write to Holy Cow! Press, Post Office Box 3170, Duluth, Minnesota 55803. Please visit our website, www.holycowpress.org.

For Cole and Ada

Table of Contents

Act 2

Act 3

Acknowledgments

Thanks to these literary journals, anthologies, and organizations for previously publishing the following poems:

Great River Review: "Diary of a First Grader," "Under a Plastic Tarp"

Low Down and Coming On: A Feast of Delicious and Dangerous Poems about Pigs, edited by James P. Lenfestey (Red Dragonfly Press, 2010): "When Pigs Fly"

Mizna: "Cutting Bread," "Adrift," "The Effects of Rock and Roll on an Unborn Fetus," "Ada Asleep/Age Three"

mnartists.org: "The Fruit"

Pinyon: "Little Witches"

St. Paul Almanac: "The Hideaway"

Turtle: "Chinook, Montana, 1992"

My thanks to the Association of Writers and Writing Programs and the writers of the Twin Cities for creating the vibrant artistic communities that sustain me; Becca Barniskis, Sharon Chmielarz, Kate Lynn Hibbard, Kathleen Jesme, Mary Jo Thompson, Susan Steger Welsh, and Morgan Grayce Willow for reading drafts of poems in writing groups; Robert Hedin for masterful editing of individual poems; Naomi Cohn, Anna Meek, William Reichard, and Valerie Volgrin for their astute and sensitive readings of the manuscript; Heather Koop for supplying personal and historical accuracy; Anoka-Ramsey Community College for giving me time; the Anderson Center for Interdisciplinary Studies, Stephanie Ash, Cynthia Cone, and Joan Drury for providing marvelous spaces to write and revise; the Minnesota State Arts Board for funding; Jim Cihlar, magician and manuscript therapist, for sculpting these pages into their final form; Jim Perlman for his patience and steadfast belief in my work; and to my family, Scott Velders, Ada Kysar, and Cole Velders, for their love and support while I completed the book.

— K.K.

Act I

Last October

The umber light		slants through leaves
like flute notes fading		against the distance.
The goose, fat and		heavy at the lake's edge,
is the weight of war		in a mother's heart,
a husk, a silence,		a muffled cry while
the light lies	undisturbed	on the horizon.

Farm House Girl

MADELIA, 1966

In the wheat fields of southern Minnesota,
the boys ran in the muddy, weedy
ditches, pants dirty, corn-colored hair
flying from their foreheads. In the woods
by the creek with tall grasses and
matted leaves, they tugged wood
to summer fires, made lean-tos
from large, leafy branches.

The little boys followed the older ones,
returned home for lunches of sandwiches,
Oreo cookies, and lemonade, and later
naps as the hot summer sun
slanted into the big farmhouse windows
shaded with calico curtains, the cotton
bedspreads soft against their sweaty heads.

The older boys sought shade, dug cool earth
with bent spoons, dumped earthworms
in rusted coffee cans for after-dinner fishing;
they chased the cattle, threw cowpies,
built elaborate trenches for plastic
army men, Germans to get
blasted with bombs of mud.

But the girl in her thin print dress
with a big bow, hair in plastic ribbon barrettes,
helped her mother chop, bake, sift, stir;
brown, braise, can, and mop; dust, scrub,
mend, sew, and scour. She did puzzles
in the darkened afternoon living room, read
books as she waited for big boys to come back.

Sometimes she went out on the porch,
called their names into the wind but heard only
the whine of cicadas, the snuffle of the pigs,
the far away lowing of cows in the field
near the woods, the wild woods
near the muddy, glistening creek.

Dream Poem

Mother, Father,
I have everything at bedtime:
a net of flowers,
a clock, a full little belly,
bed clothes made of candy wrappers,
petal wet darkness.
I am sleeping in the spirit gardens,
in these waters, quick and hot.
Will you wake me?

Diary of a First Grader

My mother drives me
to school in her pajamas,
makes me double check
my lime green backpack:
lunch bag, racing car folder,
homework on telling time,
orange hat and mittens,
green baby blankie
hidden in the front pocket.

I like to be on time,
please my teacher,
make my friends laugh.
When Mr. Scott's voice
bellows on the intercom,
I am rigid with attention.

I know how to sneak in line
for a second chocolate pudding,
grow a meal worm in oatmeal,
flour, and cornflakes.
I know reindeer eat
brownish green moss,
and llamas live in Peru.

My teacher likes us quiet
doing worksheets,
but I am looking out
the window thinking
of volcanoes and starships
zooming through space,
explosions and eruptions,
bigger than the earth to infinity.

I can tell half past two
on the grade school clock
in this room with wide
windows and white shades
pulled down with a stick.

When my mother picks me up,
she has changed out of her pajamas.
I run into her arms, eager
to tell her of my day.

First Kiss

St. Paul, 1973

Amid the ransacking rumble
of semitrailers, we stumbled

the sloped hill of Pierce Butler,
the truck route near the train tracks.

Around small trees and large bushes,
weeds sticking in our clothes,

we half-slid to a secluded spot.
He knelt, pulled me down.

Facing each other, a light press
of lips, no more than a promise,

a signature on a blank page
in light blue ink that fades

in sunlight, a slight spray
of small flowers amidst gray clouds.

The Hideaway

St. Paul, 1972

The purple tree was the color
of dust in moonlight, the bark
brown in its slow death,
the split in the branches low
enough to reach by standing
on a bike seat. Nestled in its
hollows, we'd lean back, ponder
the shimmering stars in the
darkening late summer sky,
leaves painted orange by sunset.

It was imminent:
the start of school,
the change of season,
our feet outgrowing our
beat-up summer shoes,
the bombs falling on TV.

The news was bad,
the body count climbing
my mother distraught,
my father taking his students
to peace marches, the men
in black cars parked outside
on our silent street, waiting.

That girl, running on
a flat dirt road, her naked child
body slick, smooth, and strong,
how could I share my favorite
bell bottoms and purple shirt,
ride her on my banana bike,
let her lean back into the arms
of the tree, the only flames
the sunset in the distance?

I Sit Still in Church with a Pencil

Two gazelles, brown horns curving, leap toward rocks on the dry-grassed Seringeti.
With youthful joy, they spring together, almost flying.

The old man, chopsticks in hand, confronts the sushi the wasabi, the soy sauce.
The china teacup shakes as he lifts it to his lips.

The minister weaves words into white artificial waves of oblique
faith and belief. I sit still, moving only a pencil.

Cats crawl on blackened silent streets, stealthily stepping
out of headlights into the darkness, pavement glistening.

The shopkeeper stirs the aluminum vat of milky tea, steam frothing forth,
his lined hand holding the wooden spoon. Exactness is his prayer.

Salvation

Thief River Falls, 1919

Pastor was
a towering man
with slumped shoulders
and a heavy brow.
At the pulpit,
you could not see his eyes,
just his mouth moving,
his voice loud and echoing
against the granite walls,
the polished pews.

After service,
he always held
Mama's hands,
saying life was
hard, hard, hard,
then laid a blessing
atop my head, like
patting a lamb.
I squirmed, already
uncomfortable
in tight lace-up boots
and a too small frock,
layers of petticoats,
my older sister's
worn wool coat
buttoned tight.

Some nights Mama
sent a casserole
to his small house.
I walked carefully,
the covered glass dish
between two towels.
He would try to detain
me, ask me questions,
but I would not talk,
head down, knowing
he might see my sins:

the time I scribbled in
Anna's book when I
was a toddler, the
stolen piece of pie
from the church bazaar,
the place my hand
went at night under
the cover for comfort
when I was alone.
I know he saw
through my silence.
My mother had warned
me to be polite,
so I could not leave
until excused to
run back home.

I never told my mama
how he held my thin
arms tight in his grip,
how he talked with
hot wine breath, his
face close to mine,
how I shook with fear
and almost peed
when his hands touched
the front of my dress
and cupped the space
between my legs.

I heard my shame
in his towering voice
burning. I vowed
to only speak when
spoken to, to be
kind to my younger
brother and older
sister. I vowed to
take no pleasure in
the sweet summer
peaches in the orchard,
the tall weaving grass

of the prairie, the cool
green water of the
swimming hole.

I vowed to cleanse
myself, to immerse
myself in the waters
of holy sacrifice, to
record in my diary
every day my good
deeds, to erase
my sin, to control
my hands, his hands,
his ungodly hands.

German

During the First World War,
my great-grandparents burned
all the German books except the Bible,
which they hid wrapped in canvas in the root cellar.
They would not speak German, even in hushed tones at home.
Grandma strove to e-nun-ci-ate every word clearly,
memorize English poems she could tick from her tongue
like cards in the dealer's hand. They stopped
making *strudel, lebkukken, spaztle, springerle*
and instead cooked green beans until blanched pale,
casseroles with pronounceable names ending in "hot dish"
to be served in the Methodist church basement.

During the Second World War,
there were no concentration camps in Idaho,
though *Godheilf Willhelm,* or G. W. as he was known,
feared when from his dusty tenant farm,
he saw the Japanese, and sometimes the Chinese by mistake,
rounded up. Saved by the color of his skin, if he kept
his mouth shut, his head down, the irrigation water turned
on high every Thursday, church on Sunday, and the store
on Saturday morning, they could pretend to be safe,
but at home, he hid coins in jars beneath the floor boards,
on the attic rafters, behind the canned tomatoes in the cupboard.

He was ready for another depression, another draft,
a war. He was waiting, always alert, ready, knowing
he was the little guy, knowing
the bankers owned his land, knowing
his tongue revealed his origins, knowing
politics could change, and he would once again
be the one they had to blame
to make the rest of the country feel safe.

Things I Learned from My Grandmother

Wear rubber gloves while washing dishes
      to keep your hands soft for handholding.
            Carry a file, a plastic rain bonnet, and a small packet
                  of tissues in your snap-shut purse.
                  Let the men pump the gas.

When you aren't sure what to eat for lunch,
      open the refrigerator and see "what falls out."
            Do not talk about childbirth, romance, or sex
                  until you are too old to be embarrassed by it.
                  Soft cheeks are good for kissing.

It is legal to peruse the dictionary while playing Scrabble.
      Marry a man you can beat at Pinochle.
            Men's work is outside of the home; women's, on the inside.
                  Do not let people know you can speak German.
                  Cooking does not involve spices.

Tend the flowers in your garden—peonies, roses, columbine.
      When picking raspberries with your small grandchildren,
            hang an old coffee can with the string attached
                  around your neck to keep both hands free.
                  Read Family Circus for cute things kids say.

Pay attention to what the men in Washington do with your Social Security.
      A woman's goodness is judged by the cleanliness of her house.
            Always say a visit was too short when you say goodbye.
            Do not question the doctor.
            Leave with grace.

The Effects of Loud Rock and Roll on an Unborn Fetus

He lay curled like an ear
against her belly walls, trusting
the sleeping sway of her hips,
the sigh of her motherly breath
as it moved from diaphragm to throat to mouth.
He trusted the rhythm of her words,
the pitch of her voice, the unrelenting
motion of the car in the curves of rural roads,
like a train, a cradle, a swing,
he was lulled in silence

        until
        an explosion of words, the fidgeting,
        scratching noise of her new selection,
        then the jolting bass boomed
        into his soft, tendril-like bones,
        the screeching of guitars
        and then a wailing voice
        Have you ever been experienced?

        He had been missing this life force,
        this pounding like blood in his body,
        the rhythm of his heart.
        With tightened fists, he beat
        the walls of his watery cell, opened
        his mouth to admit the salty fluids
        and practiced a silent wail,
        getting ready for his real experience.

Ada Asleep/Age Three

I etch the cellophane
whispers of her skin
with my finger:
misty soft legs,
tender muscled calves,
small foot curved in sleep.

Her small hand opens
its slender fingers,
then clasps the dream
like a cloud caught
in the tender branches
of an aspen tree.
Her dream is a river,
a rice paper painting,
the echoes of her day.

Shadows toy with her
flickering pale lids,
the red flush on
her ivory cheeks,
the curl of her ear
against her pillow,
the damp pink
glistening of her lips.

She breathes into
the crocheted quilt,
pastels that she loves,
and whispers my happiness
in her dream.

Dresses Everywhere

The presents for my baby daughter arrive
in the mail for her spring birthday,
dresses with buttons and bows, flowers
and lace, some with matching panties.
In her wide-stanced wobble,
she navigates the rooms, walking then falling,
getting caught in the hems
as she crawls forward, tries to stand again,
her pudgy white legs so vulnerable,
her diapered bottom exposed.

: :

My mother couldn't be seen in pants.
If a farmer drove down the road,
dust plume and puttering pick up
announcing his arrival,
she'd run to the barn and hide
or pull a dress fresh from laundering
off the line as she hurried to the outhouse
to change, to not be seen in pants,
my grandmother's rules about legs,
thank you notes, and hemlines
holding her tightly in her place.

: :

My elementary school
had a rule that all girls must wear dresses.
I wore thick green corduroy pants
to school to warm my legs
as I waited in line with the safety patrols,
removing them in the damp smelling
wood-paneled cloakroom, hanging them
on a blackened hook greased by the hands
of a century of children before me,
my bruised and skinny legs sticking out
of the short dress, two cold white sticks in winter.

: :

Now four, my daughter's favorite made-up song
is "Dresses Everywhere." She sings in a tuneless
voice, the lyrics changing each time.
Her dresses must be pink or purple
with bows and lace, frills, or big white collars.
At school, she rolls in grass,
makes mud cakes decorated with elm seeds,
digs deep holes in the sand
because *the dirt is so cuddly, Mommy.*
I long for the day she will prefer pants,
cover her silky long legs with dense blue fabric,
to keep her safe, protected, clean, unharmed.

Playing with Planes

I did not see the woman
fall in a final, graceful dance,
her arms at her side, legs bent.
I did not see the pair of businessmen
sweep the air holding hands,
pass towers of glass, flames, then ash.

I did not see the sobbing, soot-covered people,
the bridges covered with horrified onlookers,
the silent swarms walking north. My son
played pilot, his large, loud machines
miraculously zooming through sparkling skies
as I changed his sister's diaper.

Like children everywhere, he believes
firefighters will save him,
police officers know the way to safety,
stairways are never blocked by impassible debris,
elevators glide up and down on cushions of air,
tall buildings stand forever,
and no one he loves will ever die.

Under a Plastic Tarp

In the first days of the war,
she comes to me, her face
on the front page of my newspaper.
She is caring for her husband,
her sick six-month-old baby,
living on a rocky ledge under a sheet of plastic
outside of Baghdad. She has a dented pot,
a blue plastic bucket with dirty water,
city clothes and not enough blankets,
her breast milk getting thin as
she waits for the bombs to come and go,
white rock dust smeared on the staring
blank face of her older, wide-eyed child.

I sip my coffee. All over the world, women
are turning on burners or blowing on a few dried twigs,
flames for food, warmth, and sustenance,
not shock and awe. We linked by fire and water,
pots of steaming grain and warm toasted bread,
the hungry eyes and mouths of waiting children.

My daughter plunks down her crust
and joyously announces *I'm done, I'm full!*
She carries her plastic bunny plate to the sink,
returns to the basement to play camping
with her brother, cooking soup on a pretend fire,
sleeping on a pile of couch pillows and hairy dog blankets.
Pretending the world is safe, I close the paper
and rinse white china in a stream of clear clean liquid,
trail slow circles with the soapy sponge, haunted
by the woman under a plastic tarp.

Holding Her

In the twilight of the evening,
as the last beads of light slip through
green velvet curtains that hang like moss,
her ten-month-old body
curls itself around my middle,
her face buried in my breast,
her silken skin freshly bathed,
her limbs curved and heavy with sleep.
　　　The world holds still;
the earth stops on its axis
and hangs, complete in this pause,
the sky and moon silenced
by the breath of a sleeping babe.

Faultlines

St. Paul, 2002

At the grocery store,
the moms of Highland Park
in hastily-pulled ponytails bend
under the weight of the car seats
holding well-fed babies, struggle
to control their straying toddlers.

Stuffing bundled babies into carts,
we babble bright words, only hint
at the shadows that gather in our days:
He's having a bit of trouble toilet training.
In the checkout line, your children whining,
her tired eyes meet yours and say,
It is not your fault.

But the baby hasn't been bathed,
the preschooler watched TV
while, in a sleepless haze,
you stumbled around the house—
laundry, breakfast, wastebaskets,
mail, phone calls, laundry—
unable to focus, prioritize.

The eyes of the grocery store manager
skip over your unwashed hair, your
postpartem body. You are invisible;
you are a checkbook, a credit card,
the major household shopper.

Sometimes,
when you do get a chance
to catch the sleep that eludes you,
you think in the dark about
the untidy house, the weeds in the garden,
the fallen flowers crushed by last night's rain.
All the faults in this little world are yours,
the foundation cracking under the weight of the house,
the weight of the family, the weight you cannot carry.

Monkey on a Wire

My son first encounters death
on a nature show about monkeys
in India who live on rooftops,
urban animals allowed to play,
swinging from branches and wires,
sometimes powerlines that kill them.

He watches the funeral procession,
the precious red silk and white flowers,
the sacred animal laid out like a child.
Mommy, what's wrong with the monkey?
Why doesn't he get up?

The next day, he asks a friend
Where is your dog? He's dead, she says.
My daddy buried him somewhere in the yard.
That night, my son tells a pretend story
about his dead brother buried in the lawn—
he didn't eat enough and died

like a miscarriage, a chromosomal
mishap, red silk blood streaming,
a brother not meant to be born,
buried in the back yard of our dreams,
a bad chance, an accident, a monkey
swinging from a wire.

The Storm

Through quills of pines,
through the glory
of naked human flesh,
the broken dove beats
anger like bright curls of leaves
deep blooming, then peeling red.
This night keeps going, bearing down
on the line between spirit and self.
Rage passes over our house,
touching no leaf.

Cutting Bread

Making sandwiches in the late night house,
she cuts heavy crusted bread with a long serrated knife.
Crumbs of grain gather on the coarse wood board.
Darkness breathes in the summer windows.

A BBC voice tells of atrocities in Iraq,
heads cut from bodies, held high for the camera,
ski-masked rebels clutching them by the hair.

Above her, children and husband sleep, windows
open to the rhythm of cars passing, echoes
of train wheels on trestles, cicadas in tall grass.

The earth breathes. The bread breathes too.
She slides sandwiches into plastic bags,
presses zippers, sealing them in.
She turns off the radio and stands in starlight.

The knife on the counter by the sink,
she walks the stairs to join the sleeping.

Act 2

Bones

Two Harbors, 2009

Will Do: clean homes, cabins, etc.
reliable, reasonable rates.

Waking up at the roadside motel to see my view:
the graveyard, small rounded stones in lines,
flat insets punctuate the browning grass.

For Sale: Black sunflower seeds.

In the foreground, lines, then a sketch
of white summer sky, sizzling air,
the relentlessly blue lake.

Wanted: Vendors to sell their craft
items at Christmas in July.

Just to the north along the highway,
white amputees fall, stressed
from drought, insects, and snow.

I wish home health care, providing
Quality care for people of any age.

The delicate birch give up their bones
to pine, hardwood, purple-topped grass.

High school boy will do mowing/raking,
other yard work. Have own equipment.

What graveyard will my children wake to,
these woods gone to prairie,
animals with thin fur and quick eyes?

Clarinet lessons for any elementary
age child. Call Ariel.

We plant things neatly, using measurement,
asphalt, and lines, not a streak
of blue, a brilliance of green,
the white barked tree, breathing.

For sale: oak firewood, some birch.

Reverend Tennyson Comes to Call

MACKINAC ISLAND, 1830

We both knew why he'd come
to sip tea from chipped Wedgwood
cups, eat biscuits, slightly stale.

It was hot on my father's porch,
the one elegant part of the house.
Before she died, my mother
spent summers there and winters
at the piano she fought to keep in tune.
My father, he hated the wicker chairs,
the fineries, and my sister too stayed
in the barn with the horses, the men.

Rev. Tennyson had long, slender
hands, a nasal voice—not unpleasant,
but I loved a man who worked
the farm with my father. We'd meet
in the field, lay on a blanket together
staring at the white dazzle of clouds
against that blue summer sky, then
pick raspberries, blueberries, or rosehips.
My father knew and didn't know:
he was occupied by his trade.

The pastor was looking for a wife.
My sister was like a wild horse, beautiful
but untamed. The soft man turned his eyes
to me, but I spent my winter evenings
in the kitchen near the kerosene lamp
teaching my companion with a lesson book,
pencil stubs, and my old primer.
Sometimes we hunted near his cabin,
walked the trapline while his mother wove
baskets and beaded for trading at the post.

In the insistent afternoon sun,
Tennyson swallowed his cold tea,
stared at my gloved hand, then abruptly
left to finish his Sunday sermon.

Walking down the path, he turned,
almost spoke the burning words.
I would have told him I love another,
chose to live between two worlds
on this bounteous wooded isle.

The Ghost Husband

Her hairbrush languished on the mirrored vanity
next to her handwritten letter.
The dead one was near her again.

Behind the rocks, hidden by oak
and birch, the fire kicked up smoke.
A darkened spirit floated above the lake.

The paper rustled in the wind. The curtains shifted.
The distance between them felt endless.

Lifting into the air, a starling
fled deeply into the autumn light,
like sorrow on a leaf floating upward.

She no longer knew his name,
the touch of his beard against her face,
the softness of his cheek beside his long, straight nose.

Upon the rocks, hidden behind birch,
beyond the turtle slipping into
the still, calm lake, he lay to rest.

On the kitchen table, stale milk
and a husk of bread drying in the strange grief.
She lie on the couch, toward the wall, uncomforted.

The sweetgrass is smoking, sorrow on a leaf floating upward,
Superior's waves crashing against gray rock.
Without knowing it, they crossed the border between them.

The Day Ten People Died at Red Lake

"Are you a relative?" Don Shelby, WCCO-TV
Outside the Beltrami County Hospital
Monday, March 21, 2005

We drove the narrow road
north to the border, flashes
of blue sky, brown mud flats
packed hard with rocks, plowed
by waves with perfect precision.

With perfect precision,
he aimed at faces, heads,
sounds popping like a paint gun,
the numbers of dead counting
upward like a video game score.
Against the door leaned
a teacher and student, others
huddled in closets, bullets spraying.

Before the bodies on stretchers,
before terrified parents lined
the school fence, before
his name hummed in wires
and airwaves, he closed his mouth
on the gun and joined
the white-capped waves,
the muddied weeds in the ditches,
the dark green shade of the pines.

The day ten people died at Red Lake,
we drove a winding road north.
With perfect precision, light flashed
between the silhouettes of trees.

Ghosts singing on those stark high
wires, we will not say your names.

Kosovo Refugees

APRIL 1999

The air raid sirens.

A woman in a field,
head wrapped in a dirty cloth scarf,
bouncing a baby bundled in rags
to quiet its hungry cry.

A muddy field filled
with people in nylon coats
carrying cloth bags,
heavy toddlers in their arms.

A pregnant woman on a stretcher,
her stomach a mound of grief.

The air raid sirens going off.

A group of muddy children
inventing a game with sticks
they saved from a small fire.

Trains filled with people—heads,
arms, hands sticking through
the high windows of metal cars—
move slowly toward the border.

And the air raid sirens.

Those who stay in the town
fear the cluster bombs,
the militia in uniforms with guns.

The tent cities,
one diaper per family, water,
a blanket, a man begging a relief worker
for a piece of plastic to keep his family dry.

And the air raid sirens.

Frederica, the Aging Flamenco Dancer,
Arrives at the Eastern European Resort

Oh, I came here to spread my numb toes in the loamy dirt of the forests of Croatia, to bath in the mineral waters of this ancient resort. Roman Emperors used to steep the battle-weary dirt from their bodies here; empresses of Europe stewed in the hot springs; princes, barons, empire builders ate wild boar in the restaurants with gleaming chandeliers and white starched table clothes, candles flickering yellow light on their fat faces. Then the Communist cadres threw trash in the corners, proletariat drunkards urinated in the hallways, burnt the mattresses, and threw bedsprings from the torn-sashed windows. Now the new entrepreneurs find cheap labor: too-blonde girls with blue eye shadow languish behind the front desk; old bent men in large black suit jackets drag cardboard suitcases up the grand staircase.

I have come to entertain, dance flamenco hot enough to fire the furnace, rebuild the crumbling walls. I lounge by the door of the kitchen at lunch time in my silk morning robes. The Chinese dishwasher stir-fries his meal in a greasy wok, the smell of greens emitting from the kitchen as I eat my breakfast eggs and seared pork. The men at the large table are already drunk, handling the hostess, a slight girl not long out of school, thin and scared of their boisterous advances. Tonight when I dance, I will return their passion, my red silk dress tight against my buttocks and thighs, castanets clapping their attention, my arms poised, stiffened, head turned away, my graying hair tight against my head, black-heeled shoes pounding the wooden stage. I will rekindle the flame, stroke the heat, burn this aged palace new.

The Fruit

"Juardo said she remembers growing up believing
that women got pregnant by simply sitting next to a man."
Minneapolis Star Tribune, *Sunday, June 19, 2005*

Unlike the virgin, there was no annunciation,
no angel came unto me with a halo of light
and a thin, graceful finger pointing at my flat belly.
I thought a woman could get pregnant just sitting
next to a man. I avoided my teasing uncle's laps, stayed safe
in my circle of girls on the dusty barrio playground.

How did it get inside me? A message from the desert hare,
the whisper of the aloes, the scratch of the cactus against
the wind, the trail of the turtle through the sand, the grunt
of the desert peccary? Did God whisper his will inside me?

Was it the pit of peach I accidentally swallowed?
The apple seed that innocently slid down my throat?
Un huevo fertilized by some cock? The bull's testicles
served at my cousin's wedding? *El beso* bestowed upon me
by the priest? A cockroach crawled inside me?

I whisper with my friend Maria. We cannot ask the sisters
at the convent, and our mothers turn their heads in silence,
arms grinding corn, kneading dough for tortillas, rubbing
twisted clothes up and down corrugated washboards.

Was it a bird bringing my wish for a child, or is this the fate
of Eve like the monthly visitation? I am alone.
My stomach grows round, hard, not like a rock, but a ball,
a piñata, a soft paper skin filled with small gifts.

Inspected by Number 5

On Saturday nights, I walk arm and arm with Li Hong, to tease the night merchants, drink noodle soup, and look at clothes, radios, and ice cream.

Six days a week, we sweat in the dusty warehouse, no windows, a few lazy fans. We wipe the sweat on our sleeves and dream of Mama and Baba

in the countryside farming a bit of land. I want to try for the modern life, to get ahead, to buy a TV for Didi. No men here, only the foreman

and a dormitory are filled with girls like me dreaming rice with no pebbles, vegetables with chunks of tofu, a steamed fish, *jaozi* plump with spiced

ground pork. We live twelve girls in each room, beds stacked three high. Li Hong and I perch like birds in a tree in our private nests.

Li Hong collects letters from her grammar school sweetheart—she works for her dowry. I send small checks to Lao Jia, saving enough for vegetable dumplings for myself.

I am number five, the checker. I inspect the seams, the pocket linings, and the hem. We are making underwear and undershirts for little girls,

pink and blue patterns, pure and shining white. Will they fit just right, bringing happiness to the brown-haired girl in Italy, the golden-haired girl in Canada?

I tuck in my note, my secret message:
Inspected by Number 5.

Makinac Island/Spring Melt

After the snows melt, after the rutted roads are filled
with Superior sand by the young men from the sanitorium,

after the wagon wheels can smoothly travel,
mud melting away into green undergrowth and sprinkles

of white wildflowers and the lilacs in the yards,
there was relief as we ate our first fresh food: wild asparagus, greens,

the promises of berries flowering in sunny patches.
Out of the woods came our people who wintered in their shacks,

coming to trade their furs. Father would order extra cargo
from the Dixon. The store filled with dry goods:

pots, rough cloth, buttons, ladles, tins of meat, flour, coffee,
teas, and sugar for after the maple syrup was gone.

My sister rode far into the woods, coming home
bitten by mosquitoes, the horse itching with ticks.

I worked the counter, played the concertina for the children
outside the window, their sooted faces in rapture

while their daddies sat on the store porch smoking pipe, talking
about who died over the winter. I played light tunes,

like the little candies I slipped into their hands while their mamas
sold precious elk rugs as the beaver pelts became scarce.

They say the loggers are coming this way,
and people are moving farther into the woods,

want to keep their children close, trying to live in the old way.
The skin on my face is stretched tight in the Superior wind,

the water in the lake still cold, but the warmed sand glistens,
and in the ditches, the hope of purple lupine.

Act 3

Adrift

I dream you are having an affair.
It is unconsummated.
You gently hold her hand
in front of government centers
and art galleries,
my girlfriends driving by slowly,
long enough to glimpse
her sensible gray bob, your
long interwoven fingers.

I am not hollow, nor does anger
overwhelm me. We are drifting,
having grown familiar
with this landscape,
the way the trees bend,
the subtle shades of light
on the leaves, the beating of waves
on the lakeshore, the moonlights'
reflection on our aging faces,
the stoop of the shoulder,
the soft rounded stomach,
all this within reach, all this
that you are giving up.

Chinook, Montana/1992

The old farmhouse
below the rolling grazed field
north of the Bearpaws
lies low on the horizon.
The creek turns by the barns, beyond
two graveyards: one for machinery,
one for the tallest of trees.

We walked there, took a picture,
then lay down on the stick-filled
cool ground, our heads resting
on a log. The sun and wind
moved the poplar leaves above us.
You left so fast.

Your grandma lived in an old motel,
her housedress clean but ironed pale,
her hands warm, wrinkled, and dry.
She served soda, told me of
her grandchildren and crosswords.
You presented me as a girlfriend,
and I smiled at the fraud,
aware that she might see through it.

Your cousins, the potato salad,
the empty farm house,
the urgency with which you took me
then left me alone laying
among the twigs and sticks,
there was something wrong,
some ghost, the kindness
covering something in your family.
Perhaps that's why I don't remember.

Frankie in the Attic

Scene I / Your Parents' Attic, 1956

Next to the dusty Mason

        jars of coins, the boxes

of *National Geographics*

        wedged in the corner

the framed photo, her hair in a

        1940s pageboy, the rounded

curls at the side of the face,

        the dark-haired beauty

who haunted your father

        before he met the jaunty

stewardess, your mother,

        on her way home from Cuba.

He moved her to a small town

        never to travel again.

Scene II / My Front Porch, 2009

After it closes down/can we
still love/or is it merely the past
we see through the prism/of
each other's eyes/gray moths
beat the bare bulb with
their wings/my thoughts
dangerous, burning/ taking
me nowhere that you or I
can go/trapped now in
the small towns of our lives/

Scene III / Your Attic, 1995

L.P. albums, band posters, torn t-shirts

        musty French novels with scribbled notes.

Like an arsonist's flame,

        with unlit longing,

my question burns:

        where did/she put that child?

Scene IV / Behind a Scrim of False Romantic Gauze

you were

    a bed of lilacs,

        a naked photo in a sublet room,

art for arts sake,

           slow sketches of nude models,

                lost in the library,

    the wildest dancer contest winner,

              always reading,

       dreaming,

         staring out the window,

             thinking about the past.

Scene IV / The Gaze Lifted

You were not/at the Ramones concert
my wedding/the grocery store/biking
along the river/hiding in the woods/
repairing cars/in the small town
superette/cruising Snelling Avenue/
Susie's funeral/ that Twins game

Scene V / Your Front Porch, 2009

Sometime at parties, your children
peak around corners, looking at me

a bit too long. Did they see the yearbooks,
wonder about their fate

had you chosen someone else? And you,
in your quiet Victorian house,

picket fence and lackadaisical phlox,
clapboard and white trim,

disheveled but loved, relaxed and fun,
did you seal off that sadness somewhere?

What attic stores your desires?
What really happened/inside our hearts?

Love Poem

The thought hits me in the middle of the day:

I am your glacier over the woods, so pale.

I am your third arm, the bird

that flutters against your window

in the morning, the immeasurable cold

drawn up without a distant moon.

Somehow with stars,

we drowse like white gardenias,

a field with daisies and violets

between my throat and belly.

Listen.

I put my mouth against your heart.

Last Night's Dream/Another Love Poem

I want to be your sweetest pony,
under layers of newspapers, flour sacks, and guilt,

sprigged with violets and wild roses,
prostitutes, sky cabs, and Aussies.

I want to be your powder, your reward
for the endless round of good works and toil.

From beyond the hand throbbing
against the lock, ignoring the wrist and fingers;

from beyond an old radio, its signal faint,
the women's voices float. Walking home

under street lamps, I'm wishing you could
steal glimpses of history, art, and hunger.

The heat wave will pass.
I don't write love poems, but I'll write you.

Some days I return invisible,
holding your t-shirt against my cheek.

I want to be your Fred Durst. I want to be your
greatest fear. I want to be your sweetest pony.

Little Witches

We burn incense,
eat crackers until
salt stings our tongues,
our thirst unquenchable,
our flames unsated.

We create
animals in our bellies,
kissing pillows, stomachs,
our own religion.
We glide fingers to nipples
pointing like prayers.
Our tongues intertwine.
We form one animal,
one womb.

Japanese Garden

St. Paul, 1971

Paul Glomsky's dad was different
    than the others in my neighborhood;
        he transformed his flat-lawned yard
            into a Japanese garden with a waterfall,
                bonsai, and bamboo fencing, created
                    oil paintings in his basement, framed
                        stained glass, sculpted stone and ceramics.
                      Everything he touched was delicate,

and rowdy neighbor kids could only peer
    through the slats of the wooden fence
        for a narrowed glimpse of elegance.
            Mrs. Glomsky was plump and baked
                for her only son, round like his mother,
                    but mean and prone to average grades.
                      Once Mr. Glomsky led me down

the winding pebbled paths of his garden,
    so unlike our lilacs, crab grass, and wayward
        phlox. Thinking about him now, I wonder
            if he found joy in his graceful constructions,
                in being different,
                        alone.

Wichita Cockroaches

FOR ROBERT DANA

We were a random ragtag bunch, rejects
brought together on the barren plains
of southern Kansas, a flat town
laid out on a grid, watery beers in bars,
thirteen Titan missiles a nuclear bracelet
gleaming and winking their underground secrets
around the barren cowtown turned city.

You assembled us, shaped us with Cabernet,
poetic interrogation, and academic
confrontation. Yes, I sobbed on the balcony
after my first critique. Yes, I did not know
how to punctuate my poems. You split
a case of Chablis with me, called me your kid,
ordained me poet, and sent me on my way.

Those were lost days, r.p., before we wandered
into other jobs—selling records, working
the racetracks, writing obituaries or rhymes
for Hallmark cards. Our scruffy group
of survivors, as enduring as cockroaches,
living in the cracks and crevices,
tough and armored, inelegant and smooth,
black and dirty, getting by, surviving,
and sometimes, writing a poem.

When Pigs Fly/Kurt's Diary

April 10/

The weight of my jealousy
is unbearable. Bones behind
my eyes crack, and I wonder
who will stop these daffodils
from changing into ants.
My grandfather taught me
to eat the shells of hard boiled
eggs, but I want to hear plastic
blooming from my ears.

April 12/

The wind is starting to blow.
A storm moves in, then a clap
of thunder bursts over my roof.
I am inside, clutching a bottle.
The stove hasn't worked for days.
I am hungry for burgers, loaves
and fishes, more beer, you.

April 14/

The wolves locked up
after they delivered the mail.
I cannot move my left arm, and
flying pigs wing the bathroom air.
I'm forgetting how to survive.

The cockroaches are singing again
in the kitchen, a regular Kansas chorus
of radon and lead. I find
your message hidden under
the clothes still stinking of vomit.
You will not be coming home.

Eating Sushi with Robert Bly and Sam Hamill

MINNEAPOLIS, 2007

It took seventy-eight years to make this moment:
the cantankerous farm boy turned cantankerous poet

sitting in the large Saturday night sushi restaurant,
saki in small blue cups, tucked in a corner table, talk politics and poetry.

When the plates come, we find he has ordered beef, the only food he knew.
He asked for the brown stuff, poured too much soy in his bowl, but Sam shows him

how to chop the wasabi into the soy with sticks, dip the sushi into the sauce
that bites, stings, and barks. He tasted it all, forced the ginger flower

on to his tongue and said—*all I know is that it's not Norwegian.*

Hand Sisters

FOR HEID

Our hands trace the same path—
length of fingers, broad knuckles,
the curved nail of the thumb.
Our hands fit together as cousins
in flat, dry lands of distant buttes,
sage brush and a big wide sky
that devours birds, displays the sun
and moon as the centerpiece of all.

Our sisters' hands fit ours, hands
descended from Nebraska, North
Dakota, Idaho, flat-fielded land,
prairie land, almost desert at times.
These hands, gifts from knife-wielding
butchers, stake-pounding railroad
workers, hold our German daring,
your Ojibwe generosity and wit.

These hands are big and capable,
strong and wise, long fingers
able to grasp the words we desire
plucked from a cacophony of sounds
of flight, of light, to build the stories
that lead us back to the land,
back to our grandfathers, back home.

Early Spring: Dark Lake, 1997

The morning birds

outside the window

at the feeder

savored the rusty burnt cookie.

Chirping,

the deep brown cries

of northern winter

nearly over.

They sing

of leaves, birch,

rock, and spirit.

I get

out the map

and paintbrush, rewrite

the landscape

as it unveils in the morning light.

The birds flit

across the lake covered

with ice and snow,

edged with elms and oak,

stone and grass.   The sun and moon

seem to

touch as the pungent wind grips

the last

dream-scented house   next to the cracking ice.

The horses toss their angry yellow manes.

The land is a shell opening.

Returning to Lake Superior

In late August, stomp
on the path through
matted grass, the dark woods.

Run on the shore
and make all the stars sing.
There isn't a bud or berry
changing, moving, glistening.

Out in the open again, hear
the harp of darkness sing.
Damp air caresses your face,
strokes your snow-white feathers.

Crimson curls a leaf's edge.
A deer crosses the road
in the fog behind you.
The earth reminds you
we are all learning to leave.

At the Anderson Center

RED WING, 2006

I don't flirt with the printmaker
or look longingly at the photos
of the visiting Manchurian artist.

I eat alone, pine away the hours
with tea, ginger cookies, baths
in the steaming hot water, for
the rich baron who built this house
was long and lean and insisted
on inventing things that could fly.

Walking the river: brown bluffs,
ditch water green with duckweed
even in the cold, rabbits, red willow
woven with straw-colored vines,
the rose sunset in the eddies
of the curving pond.

Here is the moon now, almost full,
looking bitten and asymmetrical,
as if she had a hard night with her lover
but came to see me anyway. I leave
cool footprints on white winter snow.

Sure, I have a sore throat and fever,
and yes, the wine is getting to my head,
but my heart feels a happiness, drunk
and satisfied like an ancient Chinese poet.
These things are so good: the moon, the wine,
a silent place, the hills just behind the sky.

Notes

"Bones" contains excerpts taken from the *Northwoods Shopper,* Monday, May 25, 2009: 4.

"Reverend Tennyson Comes to Call" and "Mackinac Island/Spring Melt" were inspired by memoirs in *The Women's Great Lakes Reader,* edited by Victoria Brehm and published by Holy Cow! Press and Ladyslipper Press.

"The Day Ten People Died at Red Lake"—my husband worked for four years at Red Lake Hospital, next to the high school where these shootings took place. This poem is for our friends in the Bemidji area.

"Inspected by Number 5" is woven from my experience living in Guangdong province in 1996, a slip of paper in my daughter's new clothes from Land's End, and the film *China Blue,* directed by Micha X. Peled, which was shown on PBS's Independent Lens in 2007.

"Love Poem" includes some lines sampled from Rolf Jacobsen's "Guardian Angel," translation by Robert Bly, from a poetry exercise created by John Minzceski.

"Last Night's Dream/Another Love Poem"—these collaged lines come in part from poems I cut up with my Writer-to-Writer Mentor group in January 2009. Thanks to Jolene Brink, Tami Mohamed Brown, Kathryn Savage, and Annette Schiebout for sharing their words.

About the Author

Kathryn Kysar is the author of *Dark Lake,* a book of poetry, and editor of *Riding Shotgun: Women Write About Their Mothers,* a collection of essays. She has received fellowships from Banfill-Locke Center for the Arts, the Minnesota State Arts Board, the National Endowment for the Humanities, and the Anderson Center for Interdisciplinary Studies. Her poetry has been heard on Garrison Keillor's *A Writer's Almanac,* and her poems have been published in numerous literary magazines and anthologies. Kysar has taught English at Leech Lake Tribal College in northern Minnesota, Torring Amtsgymnasium in Denmark, and Beijing Normal College of Foreign Languages and Zhaoqing University in China. She served on the board of directors for the Association of Writers and Writing Programs, teaches at Anoka-Ramsey Community College and the Loft Literary Center in Minneapolis. She lives with her family in St. Paul.